# 30 Days to Transform Mentally and Spiritually

## By

## Marcus Hart

*I dedicate this book to individuals who think of change as only a long and hard process. I also dedicate this book to the Creator of this Universe, for everyday that was hard, and for everyday that was easy during my change.*

# TABLE OF CONTENTS

*Preface*

Before anyone faces death on this earth; it is a desire of both the mind and spirit to get it right. Whatever the "it" is for people to get right; you can almost guarantee it would require a pivotal change in one's own life to accomplish that desire. But how long are we expecting this process of change to take. Are we talking about days, months, or years? This frightens people immediately which causes procrastination or complete failure. Quitting being my definition of failure in this case. When an individual quits on their own life and loses their ability to realize their own potential; it is liken to the same as being a ghost on earth. This feeling is what drove me to write the book *30 Days to Transform Mentally and Spiritually.*

I wrote this book at a time when it felt like the world had refused to give me any favors or breaks. It seemed that every part of my life was completely trashed. I contemplated suicide over and over each day as the negativity around me and within me grew power over me. It was May 10, 2014 that saved my life and caused a shift in my thinking. On that day, I was able to see my three children together and spend time with them. It had been several months that passed since I was able to hear, see, or touch my kids due to unhealthy communication and relationship issues with their mothers. Before that day I thought that real and honest love in this world didn't exist. Depression and anger couldn't allow me to realize that love and happiness stemmed from somewhere that I never realized. But to understand and reach that ability to feel those two things; I would have to change both mentally and spiritually.

This book is a 30 day plan using a combination of the best quotes, biblical scriptures, and positive affirmations. I have also included my own personal poems, letters, and sayings that was compiled to put together this amazing 30 day plan to help you. I personally struggled with mental health disorders and spiritual confusion for eight years. Creating a system and plan has allowed me to overcome most of the severe symptoms and self-destructing behaviors that turned me into a ghost on earth. My plan is duplicable and simple for anyone to challenge themselves to try. Besides it's only 30 days.

The biggest struggle faced when writing this book was being able to place myself back in time to feel the hurt, disappointment, and pain all over again. The support of my mother, Angelise Hart, has offered me an overflow of confirmation on how unconditional love doesn't care about your past mistakes. I would like to acknowledge: my Divine God, Roger and Ann Johnson (maternal grandparents), Lillie and Earl Murphy (paternal grandparents), Lamonte Whitehead (father), Lolita Dixon (stepmother), Anthony Whitehead (paternal uncle), Carrie Smith (maternal great aunt), Maggie Cooper (maternal great aunt), Joyce Humphrie (maternal great aunt), Betty Greer (maternal great aunt), Steve Humphrie (maternal great cousin), my nine siblings, and my children and their mothers. I give one small acknowledgement to Krishyonna Fears; who is my ex-girlfriend. I was involved in a relationship with her when this 30 day plan was created. It was our good times and days that contributed to this system and plan working as well as it did.

# Introduction

To change the mind and spirit to cooperate for one's intended purpose, many would think it would take constant effort and years of learned skills. Constant effort and learned skills are truly part of building a foundation to allow change in one's self. However, having a plan provides more of a structured and systematic way to promote growth and change faster. There is also the ability to apply the plan to a more specific purpose or intention; such as losing weight or becoming more spiritually aware. A system or plan creates routines which can become habits or instinctual ways to react to problems. Confusion can destroy you if you are living chaotically and day by day without a system or plan that keeps your mind and spirit in complete fullness to be able to handle the pressures of life that causes mental and spiritual anguish.

In this book you will be using it as a guide for the next 30 days reading only one devotion a day as in the way you would read a tradition daily devotion. In the next 30 days you will be provided with a combination of quotes, biblical scriptures, letters, and poems. Each small devotion represents a day. This book will be best effective if the reader is able to sit and reflect for at least 10-15 minutes in silence at the beginning of the day and at the end of the day. The biblical scriptures are in no way an attempt to force people to change their religious beliefs or backgrounds as I am an ordained non-traditional minister that received my ordination from a universal church (Universal Life Church).

**30 Days to Go**

*"Do not be angry and frustrated! Do not fret! That only leads to trouble!" – Psalms 37:8 (New International Version)*

When we are angry, in a state of confusion, and worried; we are taking years off of our longevity of life. Life is less enjoyable when we are constantly feeling these emotions. Our problems are unable to be processed. This is taking away from our ability to be open to learning from the experiences we are faced with at that present moment. If you have a brain, unless you are dead there is still some level of intelligence available. You are aware and have the ability to obtain wisdom from any situation. Choose to love; because love is positive and when you give it to yourself it is felt in the body, mind, and spirit.

Repeat this positive affirmation throughout the day: "Today I press reset on everything. Today is a new day."

**29 Days to Go**

*"I press forward, who can stop the purpose and the power the universe has blessed me with."*

Declare and claim you are winning already. Within this first 48 hours of moving forward you have already shifted and changed your mind. Your spirit is willing and wanting to collaborate with your mind to get your body moving. Start thinking about how great the power of the universe is and how the energy that keeps the world and everything in perfect order does this even for you; so that your purpose is found and lived out. That in itself is the energy of love. Be open and responsive to it. You are blessed and you have no reason to feel you are being selfish for accepting the infinite power and energy of the universe to use it to benefit your happiness first. Besides it's more than enough for everyone to also have.

## Chapter 2 – The First Week

**28 Days to Go**

*"You are riding the wave of faith. The existence of life and the universe prevails again for you."*

It is time to practice smiling in the mirror while there is no one around. Study yourself closely as you smile. Think about how it feels when you are able to smile. Think about also how others will wonder how it is you are able to smile and will want to give this awesome smile of yours some attention. Your smile is contagious and this joy is your power. No one can take it unless you decide you do not want it. You have started living in faith two days ago and just like a wave in the ocean that rises higher than the level of the beach; so is your level of thinking and feeling higher. You are trusting that if you fall down that you will easily get back up. Know that the mere existence of life and the fullness of the universe is for you. It's more than enough to go around and your level of happiness is the first step to being able to live abundantly.

**27 Days to Go**

*"I am surrounded in energy and a Divine presence that is merciful to me. I am loved."*

The above sentence is also a positive affirmation. Repeat this affirmation throughout the day. Mercy on your life is a gift and a blessing. There are many who didn't live to see this moment and many more who will perish before you read the next sentence. You have unknowingly been practicing and actively displaying gracefulness since you begin your new plan. For us to take full advantage of the mercy given to us; is to simply live and smile about the fact that we have another moment. Think about gratitude today and also go outside to feel the air blow and the sun shining down on you. These miracles are happening for you. You are loved by an unseen energy and Divine presence because of the great mercy given on your life.

**26 Days to Go**

*"Life is beautiful and filled with an infinite source of love."*

Think about what the things and/or the people in this life you truly love. Think about how there must be some beauty in those things. Now look around in your house or outside and begin to notice the beautiful things that exist in this life. It is countless amounts of things on earth that are beyond amazingly beautiful. Love is tapped out of an infinite source and when we tap into it we can naturally express the love for things or people in our realities. Don't keep the love inside you trapped in a prison. Release it and begin to express it. Give praises to the fact that you love something or somebody. Now do something about it. This is active worship when we express outwardly the things or people we love. If one of those things is money, look in this life and see when money is exchanged and the beauty behind it that allows for it to be exchanged. Be a believer that when you look into the world you can see the love and beauty actively happening right before your very own eyes.

Repeat this positive affirmation: "My light shines bright. Only I can turn it off."

## 25 Days to Go

*"Moving forward with the protection and aid of positive energy and the Divine presence."*

We have a spiritual and physical nature. We all exist in our own reality, which is whatever we make it to be. We have free will, intelligence, and choices to make. There is nothing to fear although the feeling comes time and time again and can't easily be ignored. When you simply move forward for all the right reasons; positive and spiritual energy is activated for you to assist and protect you. This is done to maintain order and compliance with the natural and spiritual laws of the universe. If you are making right choices and moving forward away from your past and everything negative in your past; you are owed this protection and assistance. So far you have already jumped out of your old cycle and reality. You have activated the laws of the universe into your life and now the right situations and people will be placed in your path. You will find the right places to be at the right time because you have opened yourself to it. Whereas before you was in denial and resisting the infinite source of love freely given to you by the universe.

**24 Days to Go**

*"There are ways made out of no ways. I am blessed!"*

Repeat the above sentence as an affirmative throughout the course of your day. Think about how when you were born you came into this world with nothing but your naked body, a mind, and a spirit. Now look at the clothes you have on, the shelter you are able to have to sleep in, the ability to get to another part of the world if you so had the desire to do so. No matter how you thought previously to right now how little you have; I am telling you right now that you have more than enough to be in this present moment right now. You have added countless things and people into your life since you been born. You are rich because you have more than the average new life. Now that you know this secret, start expecting more miracles and blessings to come. When a secret gets out it creates a powerful attraction to it. Everything and everyone is drawn to it. The secret is that you are already rich and each day you are getting more than enough added. Ways are being made for you now as if it has come out of thin air. Be open to what's to come for you.

## Chapter 3 – The Suffering of Week 2

**23 Days to Go**

*"Express love like the love of the universe and Divine presence has for us."*

It is now time to step out of your comfort zone. You have already demonstrated how amazing you are in just only 7 days. If you have been applying the teachings of this 30 day plan to transform mentally and spiritually; your success may already be felt. The expressing of love starts always with you. You must feel it in yourself by being open and accepting to the fact that the presence of the Divine (however you define it for you) is effortlessly making examples of love available for you to see and feel. It has an infinite source of love that never runs out. Express love to yourself by; changing your diet, changing your self-talk, smiling, doing something you love to do that makes you feel good, and doing something with someone else that makes you feel good. This is actively participating in a life of being positive. You are making peace with the way your life has been before and safely walking away from it. Give praise to the positive energy and love of the universe by waking up and ending the day by saying thank you.

## 22 Days to Go

*"There is great mystery and power that exist in the energy of the universe that can heal all wounds, sickness, and afflictions!"*

You may have been very sick or endured an injury that left some marks before. You may have been abused, raped, rejected from others, or involved in a trauma that has hunted you since you can first remember it. You may be right now very ill and suffering from an affliction that there is no cure for. These things all have something in common. These things exist in the mind and are felt emotionally. The spirit and body doesn't even recognize what it is because the power given to it and controlling it is you. The body has to do what you tell it to do and the spirit has to dwell within you and obey your command if it wants to have an identity on earth. Both of these huge parts of us are only most effective when we use our mind (which is the strongest and toughest part of us) to tell it what to do. Both the mind and the spirit is greatly connected with the Divine presence and the energy of the universe. This is the only two parts of who we are that can travel outside time and go anywhere it wants to go. It is powerful and also mysterious. It is why I can say that if you activate positive thinking and then trust that results will come;

you can be healed. Healing can't occur until trust and faith is accepted first in the mind and then commanded by you to be activated in your body and spirit. When this transaction within you happen, you are renewed. Renewal is hope and accepting the past for what it was and moving as a new person with a new life. That is power and with great power comes the ability to overcome anything. This may hurt for a while, but trusting that healing is real will only allow the pain to exist for a short time.

Repeat this positive affirmation 7 times a day for the next 7 days: "I NOW INTEND TO EAT THOUGHTFULLY AND LIVE HEALTHY. I AM OPEN TO BEING HEALED."

## 21 Days to Go

*"The universe is perfectly made and in perfect order. I am a part of it and I will live in oneness with it."*

We know we can't live or do anything perfect. It is our imperfection that sometimes causes us the most heart break or ability to keep moving forward after making it so far. We allow our own imperfection to create these things in our mind about ourselves that aren't true. Sometimes we allow other people to plant them in our heads. If it is our own imperfection that we worry most about than why not just start becoming aware of the things that are happening perfect for us and around us to battle against the guilt trips we take so often. If you are still breathing oxygen rather through a machine or naturally; you are doing it perfectly and only you can decide to stop having access to a perfect system of staying alive. If your heart beats; it does so perfectly for you to keep you alive according to the number of beats you need per a certain measure of time. If you are able to think about anything in your mind; I am telling you that you do that so perfectly that even your most negative thoughts are on key. Isn't being honest another form of perfection? I share these examples to not point out that you are perfect; but to point out that the universe has endless perfection in it and you can connect with this perfect energy and presence. You should acknowledge to yourself that whenever you are feeling or doing something imperfect that it doesn't matter at that moment; because at that moment you are not connected with what is perfect. You also should acknowledge to yourself that when once you do connect with what is perfect that you will be better than you are at this moment. Opportunity for improvement and perfection is made available to all by the universe.

Nothing compares to this great Divine righteousness and honor shared with us.

Exercise: Breath in deeply and exhale fully 3 times. Then sit in peace and quiet for 5 minutes with your eyes closed. At the end of your 5 minutes say, "How does it get any better than this? Thank you." If you have a name for your Divine presence include it at the end of saying thank you. Do this in the morning and in the afternoon before lunch. This will open you up to receive guidance and directions for your day.

## 20 Days to Go

*"I stand in the light and I feel the love of the Divine presence and universe."*

*"Blessed are you when people insult you and persecute you and say all kinds of evil things about you falsely on account of me." –*
*Matthew 5:11 (New International Version)*

It would be wrong to deny that there isn't any negativity and darkness that exist in the world. These two things exist not to cause us to be defeated and unsuccessful, but to want more and more to stand closer to the light. The light of the world is warm, friendly, and a place where you can obtain everything you need. Everything is closed, dangerous, unwelcoming, rude, and other negativity prevails when you are in the darkness. The worst feeling is when you feel that you are in the darkness alone. The mercy, love, and providing nature of the universe and Divine presence is waiting for you to look out away from the dark and enter into the light it has. Just as walking out of a dark tunnel and stepping into the light shining outside. It is safe and nothing or no one can harm you when you constantly move to wherever the light is. Although the sun sets; the fire will burn for as long as you want it. Darkness in your life has to flee when light is placed into your life. The light is love and it doesn't need an entire area just to glow and it doesn't need power to be felt. Negativity and darkness grows and makes it impossible to see only if you stand there in it and will not move a muscle to change your ability to see. The energy and spirit of the universe is readily available to give to you what it already has prepared to give you. Just request it by walking forward out of your tunnel or dark room into a well-lit place that it has for you.

**19 Days to Go**

*"The creation work performed by the energy of the universe and the way it inspires humans; can't be described nor reproduced. It's more than magical; it's miraculous."*

The growth and development of a fetus inside of its mother's womb is truly incredible and a mysterious process. No one knows exactly how it really happens and why it happens other than knowledge of a male sperm and female egg conjoining and combining information to create life. This is just another one of the greatest miracles that can't be described or duplicated naturally the exact way with the mysterious power needed to make it work. It's a miracle which comes from a source outside of our own understanding. Receiving and retaining knowledge is also a miracle. The brain has so many ways to reason and apply logics although many try to duplicate this miracle phenomenal with a computer. If we have situations that requires a miraculous intervention, you can request it. Our purpose and who we are intended to be and have the ability to do comes from the mysterious workings of the universe. What great thing to know we can simply request the help from the energy and forces of the universe. If we request or tap into the source of all answers; then we must step out of the way. We should allow the miracle to happen naturally and not according to our own clock and knowledge. Many of us have constantly tried to bring forth our own miracles. We use outdated knowledge or techniques that aren't fit for the situation. Therefore, it is better that we allow the universe to work out these mazes for us. The solution is given for us in one or any combination of these ways: the right people sent to help, unexpected gifts, changes of your own heart or someone else's, stumbling across the right information or place, natural changes or forces in the environment that are unexplained, someone having a situation or problem that is related to yours that has found the solution to it already, someone with a different situation or problem that can have a direct impact on changing your situation or problem, someone's untimely death, a voice that is heard in your head, or a slight shift in your maturity and way of thinking. Exercise: Write out the things you want the answer to or need a miracle to happen for.

## 18 Days to Go

*"The Divine presence cringe at our sufferings while preparing restoration and peace for our better days."*

2010 Reasons to Die
To die and if I was to die would it even be based on a decision
Who truly cares and watches for my life with precise precision
20-10 and I feel back at square one again
Losing sight and it feels like the bull won't end
Reasons to go on to the last day to die
Who loves me enough to cry?
It's a minute by minute battle and I'm throwing no punches; so to
fight, I can't even try
2010 reasons to die and what's in numbers and what's in less than
glory; death?
If I die tonight let it be after I count my 2010$^{th}$ breath


When we suffer we automatically think that it is not a good thing

to suffer. We feel this loneliness cloud over us and begin to be

hunger for someone to feel as bad for us as we feel for ourselves.

The suffering becomes unbearable and we just wish it would end.

We cry, we swear, and fight against it. We rarely allow ourselves

time to just go through it and to let it past. It is said that suffering

wouldn't occur if the calculations of the universe wasn't properly

calculated. Then how would it not be the perfect time for us to

suffer? What we can't bare would not arrive at our door to take us

on the ride of suffering; if we wasn't ready for it. It is something we

all must go through. The great news is that we are so loved by the

energy and forces of this universe that it feels our periods of

suffering. Just look at days that are gloomy, rainy, or unpleasant.

This is the universe responding to what we are going through as individuals and as a whole. As the universe responds it has already worked out the exit plan and prepared the celebration gifts. The Divine presence wants to see us happy and prosper in our lives. When we come to the point where we can just accept the suffering for just that time period in our lives; we then will continue to be stronger and able to stand brave for the next short round of sufferings. If we were to stretch out all of the key events of our lives, we would find more positive, funny, fun, and happy moments then short periods of sufferings.

Applied Wisdom: Next time you are feeling like you are suffering, thank the Divine presence for not leaving you alone and for giving you strength to endure the moments you are faced with. Do this in the morning, middle of the day, and at night before bed until you start to feel lighter or pressure relieved.

Health tips during times of suffering: Increase your water intake (preferable warm water), avoid coffee and other sweet or caffeinated drinks (replace with tea and honey), apply warm towels to your stomach and head before you go to sleep, reduce the amount of meat you are eating (replace with fruits and vegetables), reduce the amount of bread you are eating (replace with crackers), reduce your dairy intake (replace with lactose free products or soy), take showers and baths regularly, brush your teeth, wear clothes that are vibrant in color, listen to upbeat music, take a walk outside, attend social functions (once you begin to feel lighter), and take a different route to places you travel to regularly, if possible.

**17 Days to Go**

*The Divine presence and the energy of this universe is bigger and outside of this life we know."*

We are sometimes so accustomed to seeing only the environment we grew up in or live in. We can easily lose awareness from only seeing just a microscopic size of what the Divine presence maintains perfect order for. The amount of energy and force needed to provide for all the known and unknown universes is beyond infinite and powerful knowledge. If we are only a tiny piece of its existence; surely the energy and Divine assistance we need is minor. We confuse our problems as being too big for ourselves and anyone else to handle. This is a terrible mistake and deception we create in our minds and should be avoided at all costs. To know energy and power exists that is infinite and unlimited and is available to anyone;

is an insult to your existence and the existence of the Divine presence when you reject this. Show gratitude for this and celebrate in praise that your purpose in this life can personally be assisted and achieved by developing an oneness relationship with the power and energy of the universe.

Repeat this positive affirmation throughout the day: "I AM NOW CREATING HIGHER SELF-ESTEEM AND CONFIDENCE."

Chapter 4 – Adjustment at Week 3

**16 Days to Go**

*"The power and positive energy of the universe doesn't exist because we believe. It's only when we develop a personal relationship with the source of this infinite power and energy when we notice and see the work being performed in our lives."*

We find it hard to trust and believe in people or things. What we are actually saying is that we do not trust ourselves and our own abilities, intentions, or our future. These bad seeds we plant in our head will not feed us anything good. We are only robbing ourselves from the great and positive things that are available to us. We look for reasons to not accept what's been available for us to enjoy. The worldly and material things such as great food, clothes, fancy transportation, and music are all available to us and was made for us. It wasn't made to just wish or acknowledge and walk away from them. These things enhance our lives and should be enjoyed. Happiness, peace, and love are the freest things you could ever find. You don't have to live in a big city, a big farm, or in the desert to obtain these great gifts that are always available to us. We should always run a check to find what it is that gives us happiness and peace and how love is most felt for us. There's no human made law that can truly stop a person from discovering what makes them happy, at peace, and loved. You have completed two weeks of this plan and if you haven't started enjoying life and celebrating to a great Divine presence we have; now is the time. Without even thinking about it you have already developed a stronger spiritual awareness and have created a new relationship with your Divine presence. You are more accepting to considering the changes made around you from applying the principles and techniques learned in this plan. You are actively participating with the plan and becoming one with who you are. This is what the Divine presence and positive energy of the universe wants for you. Your identity and acceptance of you shows gratitude for the continuous push of force and energy on your life. You have expressed love and respect for yourself and the universe by making a drastic change day by day. Surely, you didn't know that you were this cool and unique. Truth is that you are absolutely awesome and the Divine presence sings in joy whenever you are at your best.

Exercise: Prepare a meal or go out to a fancy restaurant alone. Eat the meal slowly and notice the environment and the care taken to prepare the meal. Notice how the meal is chewed and swallowed. Really taste each flavor while closing your eyes. Welcome all blessings and positive energy as you are enjoying this meal. Keep your feet flat on the floor the whole time while sitting upright. A warmness should come over your body and a moment of peace and contentment.

**15 Days to Go**

*"The universe already knows and feels your heart and inner thoughts. Therefore you were pre-qualified to partake in becoming one of the universe's best creation."*

We will never all agree on as to who is the absolute best in anything. But we can always agree that there are a collection of the best out there. To be one of the best is just as great as being the best. You are being the best at your life and there's no other competition. No one can live or think about your life the way you can. You are uniquely designed to be a master at the life you are living. You may seek out help, but not even the best advice can compete with how you best know how to use the information put in your head or on your heart. When you petition the universe and allow it to work for you, your steps will be better directed and guided away from the things your mind or heart can't handle. This is because you are the limited design edition of the universe and it knows you better than you. Knowing who you are is an endless journey and education that no degree on earth can measure against. No one can predict you if you don't want them to. This is powerful and worth applying. Your destiny will be best found when you come to the realization that you are trusted with a power that is great and inside of you. This power is unique and greater than what your mind can even comprehend. This creates confidence and the ability to just know that everything you make your mind up to want can be manifested. Never doubt the Divine presence, surrender to it and apply what you were born with. Repeat this positive affirmation for the next 7 days: "I am attracting an abundant lifestyle with ease and joy. What are the other possibilities?"

**Less than 2 Weeks to Go**

*"Follow all things that are positive and of spiritual nature in the way of all abundance and prosperity."*

*"You live longer once you realize that anytime spent being unhappy is wasted." – Ruth E. Renkl*

We are sometimes fooled into being accustomed to negative things that are projected to us on television and amongst our friends. We have to be careful in what we follow and in the things we participate in. There in the world lies lots of opportunity to gain information and to engage in activities, but these things can be destructive to our mind and spirit. We are a delicate species that are prone to fall into negative traps and self-destructive behavior. We do this sometimes as a way to avoid pain, temporary struggle, or attention and thrill seeking. We must begin to understand that are many alternative ways that are positive to fill our empty emotional, sexual, and intellectual appetites. Positive involvement with positive people and activities can provide you with so much support and place you on a fast track towards success. When making a drastic change in your life such as with following and applying the principles of this plan; it is very easy to get distracted by things that don't compliment your routine and progress.

Exercise: Begin to listen and watch inspirational and motivational songs, movies, TV shows, speeches, and clean comedy. Read books that educate you for assisting you in shaping your purpose and chosen career field that you will have a passion for. Attend network and social groups filled with people who share similar interests and values as you. Find a spiritual advisor or life coach that will keep you on track.

**13 Days Left to Go**

*"Energy and power of the universe makes life fair each day by providing fresh air to breathe. Give thanks for this."*

Sometimes it is hard to see the fairness in life when there seems to be so much injustice and prejudice in the world. These things only exist if you expect them to exist and when commanding it as a reality. We tend to forget that the order of the universe and its laws are always fair. The fact that we are given the same amount of fresh air, sunlight, hours, and body organs, just to name a few; says a lot about how fair life really is. To receive justice and to get an edge in a world where being and staying competitive to get ahead in life is encouraged; you must first be thankful that the universe already blessed you with an equal opportunity when you woke up. Perception and opinion of the world is not for you to fix, but for you to change.

Exercise: To lower your feelings about injustice, for a whole day simply just say hi and smile to everyone you encounter.

## 12 Days Left to Go

*"Your purpose is bigger than what you can see."*

It is very easy to accept the feelings of being unimportant or too small to contribute to the overall agenda of the universe. This is a mistaken feeling that you must get rid of right away. Your birth and existence would almost have to be a total mistake for your life to not matter to the Divine presence and universe. However, there are no mistakes and all things happen and work for a greater good and purpose. Just as in a car; the smallest screw or part could interrupt the perfect drivability of a car. The same is true about you. You may not see it or notice it but the call on your life to find your true purpose depends on the advancement of humility and the perfect order of the universe. Nothing or no one must be wasted, especially one's life. We are all connected by the same energy and power that keeps the perfect order of the earth. The perfect example is when a friend ask another friend to attend a funeral of someone that friend was close to. Because of the power of sympathy and empathy that friend who didn't even have a relationship with the deceased; will experience similar feelings of sadness liken to others in the room. Our connection with one another is powerful and therefore we must realize our importance and find out how we should be contributing to the workings of the universe.

Repeat this positive affirmation: "I am living towards my bigger purpose. I am important and loved."

**11 Days Left to Go**

*"The earth will shake to ensure the goals of the universe and life is willed into existence."*

*"Expect the best. Prepare for the worst. Capitalize on what comes." – Zig Ziglar*

The goals of the universe is perfect and for the benefit of our good. These goals can't be lies because the universe is perfect and doesn't register with what is not according to its natural and spiritual laws. When things are looking like they are not going as planned, we have to be able to calm ourselves to know that things are being worked out at all times for our benefit. Sometimes it will not be worked out as fast, in a certain order, or with the people we had in mind. The spiritual and natural laws only use formulas, people, and steps that comply or fit the criteria for what needs to be accomplished. For example, you couldn't use the criteria for enforcing the abortion law to punish a person that has been caught with the possession of cocaine. These two laws has different explanations and applications, therefore can't fit any other crime outside of its own definition. Likewise, there are certain spiritual and natural laws that must be applied and defined to make come into existence a desire or thought. If it means a tornado must be used to bring about community efforts to improve their buildings or relocate people to a place where they can thrive better in their life; the power of the universe and Divine presence wills it to be.

## 10 Days Left to Go

*"The best design has been planted in all of us; use it!"*

Our potential can't be measured or determined just by looking at each other. What's inside of us is a portion of the same miracle power and information that is ancient past and outside of time. We contain supernatural and natural energy properties that gives us the ability to think, reason, feel, imagine, and create. We can think of things we want and create it into existence. The bible in the book of Genesis, best describes us as being made in the image of God. An image is an exact replica of what already exists or use to exist. Furthermore, it would be absolute fair to say that if we are a scaled down version of an infinite intelligence and power; we possess this same power within us but scaled down to where we won't be

overtaken by it because of our capacity of understanding, brain size,

and physical and spiritual strength.

Read and repeat this scripture:

*"For I know what I have planned for you, says the Lord. I have*

*plans to prosper you, not to harm you. I have plans to give you a*

*future filled with hope." – Jeremiah 29:11 (New International*

*Version)*

Chapter 5 – Spiritual High in the Last Days of Change

**9 Days Left**

*"The Divine presence and the energy of this universe gives mercy to those who are faithful to connecting with it power."*

As we draw closer to completing this plan you will notice almost a repeat of what was mentioned in other places of this day by day plan. This is because repetition is the mother of all skill and also to place very important emphasis on certain key points. These points should be remembered and applied with diligent effort. Mercy is only given to those who faithfully are seeking to connect with the power of the Divine presence and energy of the universe. This oneness allows you to tap into the assistance, guidance, and protection you need for your journey and to fully live out your purpose. Dr. Francis Schaeffer once said, "It will be a terrible mistake to put any creative thing in the place of the [Divine] creator." Better to align ourselves with a power and energy that is higher than ourselves so that we may have favor in all things and all areas of our life.

Exercise: Say this as a prayer alone and in quiet, "Divine God and energy of the universe, I request your guidance, peace over my life, and blessings. Help me to choose things that will bring me closer with your presence so that I am better used to fulfill my purpose to contribute to your Divine will."

**8 Days Left**

*"In every final and good word there is always hope."*

*"Too many of us are not living our dreams because we are living our fears." – Les Brown*

Many of us are guilty of always looking for the true meaning behind every spoken word or promise. We have allowed fear and lack of trust in what the future will bring to miss every opportunity and message of hope that is beneficial to our lives. We rather give chances to things that look good rather to something that has potential or can't be seen or explained. As mention in another part of this plan, we must be careful in the physical and worldly things that we find ourselves participating in. We may be unknowingly attracting negativity into our lives. If we lean more on just simply hoping for the best in everything and everyone, then the universe will repay us double or three times more back. That same hope will be found in us and our dreams by someone else. Allowing yourself to be vulnerable and open is the only way to gain experience, knowledge, and wisdom. Jesus Christ spoke of having the same humble heart and lowly mind as a child. Our blessings will come more sooner because then we can remove ourselves from the calculations that's needed by the power and energy of the universe. Exercise: The next opportunity someone approaches you about, if it be of positive and good nature; be open to check it out.

**Less than a Week Left**

*"If we will allow ourselves to be weak and humble, the power of the universe will build us into strong spirits with good hearts."*

This same way of thinking was just mentioned previously. So it is of great importance to study this carefully and apply it immediately to your life. Review the previous day plan 7 times. Activity: Fast for the first half of the day until sundown. Eat only fruits and vegetables. Drink only water or tea. For a snack only eat popcorn. Listen to no music containing lyrics. Watch no television and don't engage in any conversation that isn't positive. Meditate for 20 minutes at the end of your fast and take a warm shower or bath before bed.

**6 Days Left**

*"Keep praising your successes and the Divine presence."*

*"Success is what happens after you survive all your mistakes." –*
*Unknown*

We tend to lock in on all of our failures and mistakes more than our smallest successes and progress. We slow ourselves down and take the attention off of what works and belittle the power and positive energy that has been blessed to us even during our mistakes and failures. Each day we should be training ourselves as if the real situation or scenario is actually happening. When the scenario or situation happens then we will view it as practice. This allows us to celebrate getting through it and learning from the experience to apply it for the future. This concept can be applied to any situation of life. Give praises most importantly to the Divine presence for allowing you the opportunity and moment; and for blessing you with the wisdom, intelligence, and skills necessary to apply for your purpose.

Challenge: Do what you would do if you were in an actual situation of your desire. If you are desiring to own a business of some sort. Set up an area of your house as your office, restaurant, day care, etc. Then perform transactions as if the business was already in existence. Notice your mistakes made and ask your customers what you can do to improve. Maybe you want to find your dream girl or guy. Get dressed up as if you are ready for a date and go to a place where you and your potential mate has a similar interest. When he or she shows up you will be prepared to have something to talk on. For all other desires, the same applies, just pick out one simple action you can do to make it real.

**5 Days Left**

*"The comfort and nurturing energy of the Divine presence is available for you who fear the unknown future."*

*"Life is tough. It's even tougher if you don't value your resources, bridges, and those who pray for you."*

As mentioned earlier and throughout this day by day plan, we have support that is stronger than any opposition, including the opposition we create in our own minds. We can be our biggest fan or our worst enemy. Fear is the most common blockage and it feeds off every possible negative assumption about something that hasn't even occurred. It makes all negative things become real. It is reported that most bad spirits feed off of our emotions. Babies are similar in this matter. Continuous negative energy and an environment of negativity can be destructive for that babies' upbringing and development. It is important to remember that we have a friendly and approachable Divine presence that is willing to comfort you in all your fears to strengthen you with courage.

**4 Days Left**

*"We are more than special if we are uniquely designed in the same way the universe was perfectly created."*

*"Do not repay anyone evil for evil; consider what is good before all people." – Romans 12:17 (New International Version)*

This point can be associated with the saying, "Do unto others as you would want them to do unto you." It is true that if we destroy the walls we build between us and other people that we will be more accepting to the fact that we are all perfectly designed the same way; just with small subtle differences. Human beings started together at the beginning of time and relied on each other heavily for survival. We must return back to this unity and collaborative effort to bring forth harmonious cooperation for change. Stand up as a leader and be the example and light everyone needs to mimic.

Repeat this positive affirmation throughout the day: "I am uniquely designed for the universe. I am accepted by those who are also wanting my acceptance. How does it get any better than this?"

## 3 Days of Work Left

*"Spirits of positive nature will be sent to destroy negative forces that come against you on your behalf. Don't worry."*

*"If you are not dying to live, you are just living to die."*

Rather you believe in angels, positive energy, or spirit guides; the universe has a spiritual presence that believes passionately about protecting us against evil or negative forces. Even in death we are guaranteed even a justified purpose and reason for our unpredicted check out time. All things of the supernatural and spiritual power are a mystery. When we reach certain spiritual highs we can feel this energy radiate through the environment and within our bodies. Our own spirit has travel capabilities and has been rumored by many to take small exits out of our bodies to explore the universe. Our mission and purpose on our lives matter and order will be maintained to protect it. It is only us who may choose to not cooperate with the flowing energy and Divine presence that intends only on blessing us with good things.

Exercise: Reread chapter 1 three times all the way through. Meditate for 10 minutes while reflecting on the words read.

## 1 Day of Work and a Wake up Left

*"The Divine presence is never late in our sorrows and*
*circumstances."*

*"Rest a restless heart."*

When we are so close there are times when we may fall short or worry ourselves away from the finish line. We place so much heart and emotion into things or people that we can become attached to. When we are forced to detach from these people or things we are drowned in our own tears and suffocated in depression. We have made it this far and now we understand that with anything that we engage ourselves in; that we must also be responsive to our mental thoughts and sensitive to our spiritual nature. The Divine presence is always ready to play the role of cleanup for our sorrows and sufferings. But we can lessen unnecessary suffering by allowing ourselves to be lead and guided by the energy and forces of the universe and Divine presence.

Exercise: Allow yourself to feel whatever pain you haven't experience for one hour. Afterwards, request from the universe that is recycled from your heart and head. Then, sit in complete silence with your hands over your heart while your eyes are closed. Do this once a month.

## 24 Hours Left

*"When trouble enters in our lives the power and energy of the universe and Divine presence has an exit plan that includes a blessing package."*

Sometimes we commit ourselves to something without planning an exit plan or a way to recoup what was lost. This happens a lot in failed relationships, college, and a job or business. Trouble or circumstances can attack us at any given moment. This isn't to say that we should expect it. However, we should always be ready to be open for change and trust in the Divine presence's ability to have a great exit strategy for us to safely remove ourselves from trouble and negativity that could cause us harm. The Divine presence also has a way of providing us with a way to get back the time, emotion, money, and effort put into whatever was started and then stripped away. Our happiness is always the centerpiece of what brings joy and harmony in the energy of the universe. Therefore, we can be assured that we have something over our lives that is better than life insurance.

Tip: Get in the habit of developing a good written exit strategy for anything you may involve yourself in. Request that the Divine may guide you in shaping this strategy.

**30 Days COMPLETED**

*"Now if the protection and aid of the Divine presence and positive energy of the universe has gotten you this far; why not savory in the victory now. Today at this moment live blessed."*

We have made it through our plan and we now have a complete system that we can review and use at any period of our life when we feel that we need to start fresh. The beauty of being blessed with new moments and days is that you always are given a chance to get right and start living the way you were born to live. As a non-traditional Christian my Divine God is the creator and CEO/Founder of this universe who gave all of the members of his organization the same lawyer, counselor, new member representative, and friend that we all share; his son, Jesus Christ. That is my belief but it's also my duty and purpose as a member of this universe to love, inspire, and properly represent and model what the power and energy of the universe can do for a person's life when you trust fully in its ability and possibilities. I know we all were created the same. But there is a bigger purpose and reason why we all have small subtle differences and abilities. That shouldn't separate us but should unite us more so that we can achieve our full potential as a universal community and as individuals. Celebrate life, for it is truly a blessing and we are both recipients and the ambassadors for blessings. The hardships are all felt the same, therefore we need to reach out more to be a representative of the caring and loving support the Divine gives to us all. When we are at our best, we can celebrate and party at our best. There is more than enough of anything available to us because we are here because of many infinite and powerful possibilities.

BE BLESSED IN THE READING AND APPLICATION OF THIS BOOK.

LOVE, PEACE, AND BLESSINGS.

# Appendix A – Correspondence

www.marcushartandassociates.com

Twitter: www.twitter.com/RealMarcusHart

Facebook Fan Page: www.facebook.com/marcusharthelps

Instagram: www.instagram.com/realmarcushart

YouTube:

www.youtube.com/channel/UCtH7bhr6qqgoxJoXk3WCXNg

Email: marcushart414@gmail.com or

support@marcushartandassociates.com

Write to:

Marcus Hart

Attn: Star Supporter

10240 W National Ave

West Allis, WI 53227


Previous and Future title(s):

My Name is Specialist Marcus Hart

Published in 2007 by Xlibris

Think Possible. Be Possible.

To be published 2015 by Xlibris


30 Days to Transform Mentally and Spiritually (motivational CD)

To be published 2015 by Marcus Hart Publishing Corporation

www.ingramcontent.com/pod-product-compliance
Lightning Source LLC
Chambersburg PA
CBHW071437040426
42445CB00012BA/1384